MEL BAY'S

HYMNS FOR AUTOHARP ®

by Meg Peterson

AUTOHARP HYMNAL or
GOSPEL SONGS ON THE AUTOHARP®*

Gospel music is rooted in the folk tradition of America. It is music from the heart and soul and appears wherever people gather to express their spiritual joy.

Folk instruments such as the guitar, banjo, mandolin, ukelele, and Autoharp lend themselves to this kind of group singing. They can provide simple accompaniments or carry the melody in a small group or a full fledged revival. Notice how well the Autoharp blends in with the spirit and harmonies of these hymns.

*The term Autoharp is a registered trademark in the United States & Canada of Oscar Schmidt-International, Inc.

Meg Peterson

When you think of the Autoharp, you naturally think of Meg Peterson. She is truly an expert on the instrument. Meg, in addition to being a fine musician, is a joyful person to work with. We are very pleased to present this fine collection of Christian Music uniquely arranged for Autoharp.

Bill Bay

CONTENTS

Figure 1

Figure 2

Figure 3

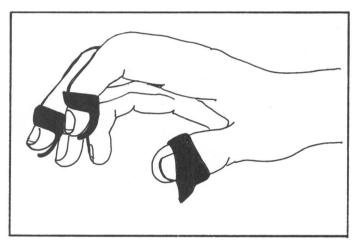

Figure 4

PLAYING INSTRUCTIONS

The first section of songs is chorded for simple strumming. This is done by placing the Autoharp on a table or your lap as in fig. 1, or holding it Appalachian style as in fig. 2. You may also choose to set your Autoharp on a table. (Figure 3)

Firmly press down the designated chord bar key with a finger of your left hand and stroke the strings to the right or left of the chord bars with the thumb of your right hand. If you are left-handed you will press with your right hand and stroke with your left. A felt, plastic, or thumb pick can be used (see fig. 4).

Always check the location of the chords to be used in each song before starting to play. The letter above the music indicates the chord to be depressed. Each slash (/) means to repeat the previous stroke in the rhythm of the song until the chord changes. Chords in parenthesis ( ) are optional. If such a chord is not available on your Autoharp, continue to use the previous chord until the change occurs.

Photos by Charles McCue

Figure 5

Figure 6

STROKING CHORDS

When stroking the chords on the Autoharp, you may want to stroke the right side of the chord bars (Figure 5) or you may prefer the sound obtained by stroking on the left of the chord bars. (Figure 6)

JUST AS I AM

JOY IN HIM

Chords used: G, C, D7, A7, D, & (Em)

Bill Bay

1. Joy____ in Him,____ there is joy____
2. Peace

____ in my soul.____ Fill - ing us now____ with His

joy____ With Christ there is joy in my soul.____

PRECIOUS MEMORIES

Chords used: G, C, D7, A7, Am, D, & (Em)

J.B.F.Wright

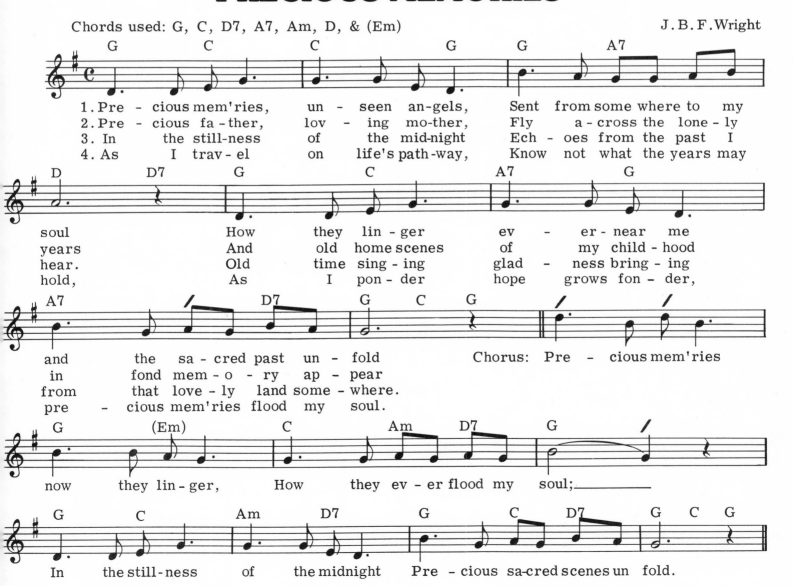

1. Pre - cious mem'ries, un - seen an-gels, Sent from some where to my
2. Pre - cious fa -ther, lov - ing mo-ther, Fly a - cross the lone - ly
3. In the still-ness of the mid-night Ech - oes from the past I
4. As I trav - el on life's path-way, Know not what the years may

soul How they lin - ger ev - er - near me
years And old home scenes of my child - hood
hear. Old time sing - ing glad - ness bring - ing
hold, As I pon - der hope grows fon - der,

and the sa - cred past un - fold Chorus: Pre - cious mem'ries
in fond mem - o - ry ap - pear
from that love - ly land some - where.
pre - cious mem'ries flood my soul.

now they lin - ger, How they ev - er flood my soul;____

In the still-ness of the midnight Pre - cious sa-cred scenes un fold.

SING TO THE LORD

Chords used: C, F, G7, E7, D7, A7, Am, & (Em)

Bill Bay

1. Sing to the Lord, Bless His Ho - ly Name._____ De-
2. Give to the Lord, Glo-ry due to Him_____

clare His glo - ry to all peo - ple.
Wor - ship Him in hol - i - ness._____

For the Lord is Great and to be feared a - bove all
Let the heav'ns re - joice now and Let the earth feel glad - ness

Sing to the Lord your prai - - - ses e-ver more.
For He shall to judge with

right-eous-ness and truth._____

© 1973 by Mel Bay Publications, Inc.

SONG OF PRAISE

Chords Used :
Dm, Gm, A7, & C

By Bill Bay

1. Sing prai - ses un - to Him Glo - ri - fy Him ev - er
2. I praise you O my Lord, Glo - ry be to you on

more Trust in Je - sus Christ!_____
high, Bless you ev - er - more!_____

E - man - u - el, Bless - ed Sav - i - or, Prince of_____ peace.
I wor-ship you and a - dore you with all___ my heart.

Christ Je - sus is my Lord I shall tell of Him where - ev - er I go.
Christ Je - sus, Lord and King. I lift up my voice your prai - ses to sing.

©1973 by Mel Bay Publications, Inc.

8

HIS BANNER OVER ME IS LOVE

Chords Used : G, C, D7, G7, & Am

WHERE HE LEADS ME

Chords Used : F, B♭, C7, F7, & G7

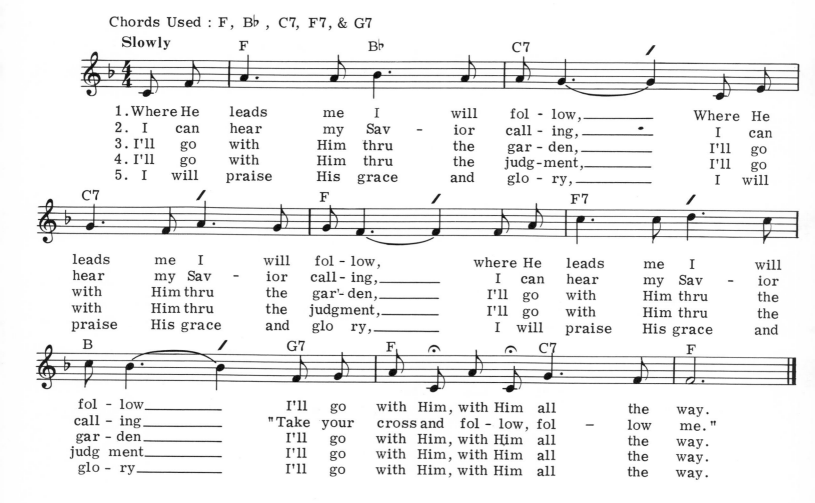

1. Where He leads me I will fol - low,_____ Where He leads me I will fol - low,_____ where He leads me I will fol - low_____ I'll go with Him, with Him all the way.
2. I can hear my Sav - ior call - ing,_____ I can hear my Sav - ior call - ing,_____ call - ing_____ "Take your cross and fol - low, fol - low me."
3. I'll go with Him thru the gar - den,_____ I'll go with Him thru the gar'- den,_____ gar - den_____ I'll go with Him, with Him all the way.
4. I'll go with Him thru the judg - ment,_____ I'll go with Him thru the judgment,_____ judg ment_____ I'll go with Him, with Him all the way.
5. I will praise His grace and glo - ry,_____ I will praise His grace and glo ry,_____ glo - ry_____ I'll go with Him, with Him all the way.

WE'LL GIVE THE GLORY TO JESUS

Chords used: C, F, G7

We'll give the glo-ry to Je - sus, And tell of His love, and tell of His love; We'll give the glo-ry to Je - sus, And tell of His won-der-ful Love._____

* Delicate upstrokes with the thumb in the middle octave or section keep the rhythm going. In contrast, stroke each chord change with a slight accent in the lower octave.

HEAVENLY SUNLIGHT

Chords Used : C, F, G7, C7, A7, B♭, & Dm

Henry Zelley
and George H. Cook

1. Walk-ing in sun - light all of my jour - ney, o - ver the
2. Shad-ows a - round me, shad-ows a - bove me, ne - ver con -
3. In the bright sun - light, e - ver re - joic - ing, Press-ing my

moun - tains thru the deep vale_____ Je - sus has said, "I'll ne - ver for -
ceal my Sa - vior and Guide._____ He is the light, in Him is no
way to man-sions a - bove;_____ Sing-ing His prai - ses, glad-ly I'm

sake thee" prom-ise di - vine that nev - er can fail._____
dark - ness e - ver I'm walk - ing close to His side._____
walk - ing, walk-ing in sun - light, sun-light of love._____

Heav - en - ly sun - light, heav - en - ly sun - light, flood-ing my

soul with glo - ry di - vine Hal - le - lu - jah! I am re -

joic - ing, Sing-ing His prai - ses, Je - sus is mine!_____

ALL WE NEED IS JESUS
(21 CHORD MODEL)

Chords Used : C, Em, Am, F, Dm, G7

Moderate easy tempo

Bill Bay

1. All we need is___ Je - sus. Fill us
2. All we need is___ Je - sus. Grant us
3. All we need is___ Je - sus. Guide us

with your___ love. Dwell with - in our___
u - ni - ty. king - dom, Pow'r and the
through each___ day. Fill us with your___

hearts Man - na from a - bove.___
glo - ry. Liv - ing Trin - i - ty.___
Spir - it. Lead us in Thy way.___

I'M SO GLAD JESUS SET ME FREE

Chords Used : G, C, D7, A7, Am

Joyfully

1. I'm so glad, Je-sus set me free. I'm so glad

Je-sus set me free. I'm so glad that Je-sus set me free, Sing-ing

Glo - ry Hal - le - lu jah!___ Je - sus set me free!

2. I'm so glad, Jesus lifted me. etc.

3. I'm so glad, Jesus cares for me. etc.

4. King of Kings, Jesus is to me, etc.

5. Lord of Lords, Jesus is to me, etc.

6. Repeat verse 1.

'TIS SO SWEET TO TRUST IN JESUS

Chords Used : G, C, D7, D, A7, Am, (Em)

Tenderly

1. Tis so sweet to trust in Je - sus, Just to take Him at His word,
2. O, how sweet to trust in Je - sus, Just to trust His cleansing blood,
3. Yes, 'tis sweet to trust in Je - sus, Just from sin and self to cease,
4. I'm so glad I learned to trust Thee, Precious Je - sus, Sav - ior, friend;

Just to rest up on His prom - ise, Just to know "Thus saith the Lord"
Just in sim - ple faith to plunge me Neath the heal - ing cleans-ing flood!
Just from Je - sus sim - ply tak - ing Life and rest and joy and peace.
And I know that Thou art with me, Wilt be with me to the end.

Je - sus, Je - sus, how I trust Him! How I've proved Him o'er and o'er

Je - sus, Je - sus, pre - cious Je - sus! O for grace to trust Him more!

PASS ME NOT

Chords Used : G, C, D7, & A7

By Fanny Crosby
and William Doane

Moderately

1. Pass me not, O gen - tle Sav - ior, Hear my hum - ble cry;
2. Let me at a throne of mer - cy Find a sweet re - lief;
3. Trust - ing on - ly in Thy mer - it Would I seek Thy face;
4. Thou thy spring of all my com - fort, More than life to me!

While on oth - ers Thou art call - ing, Do not pass me by.
Kneel - ing there in deep con - tri - tion Help my un - be - lief.
Heal my wounded, bro - ken spir - it, Save me by Thy grace.
Whom have I on earth be - side Thee? Whom in heav'n but Thee?

Chorus

1.2. Sav - ior Sav - ior, Hear my hum - ble cry;
3.4. Je - sus, Je - sus,

While on oth - ers Thou art call - ing, Do not pass me by.

SWEET BY AND BY

By S. F. Bennett
and J. P. Webster

Chords Used : G, C, D7, A7, Am, & (Em)

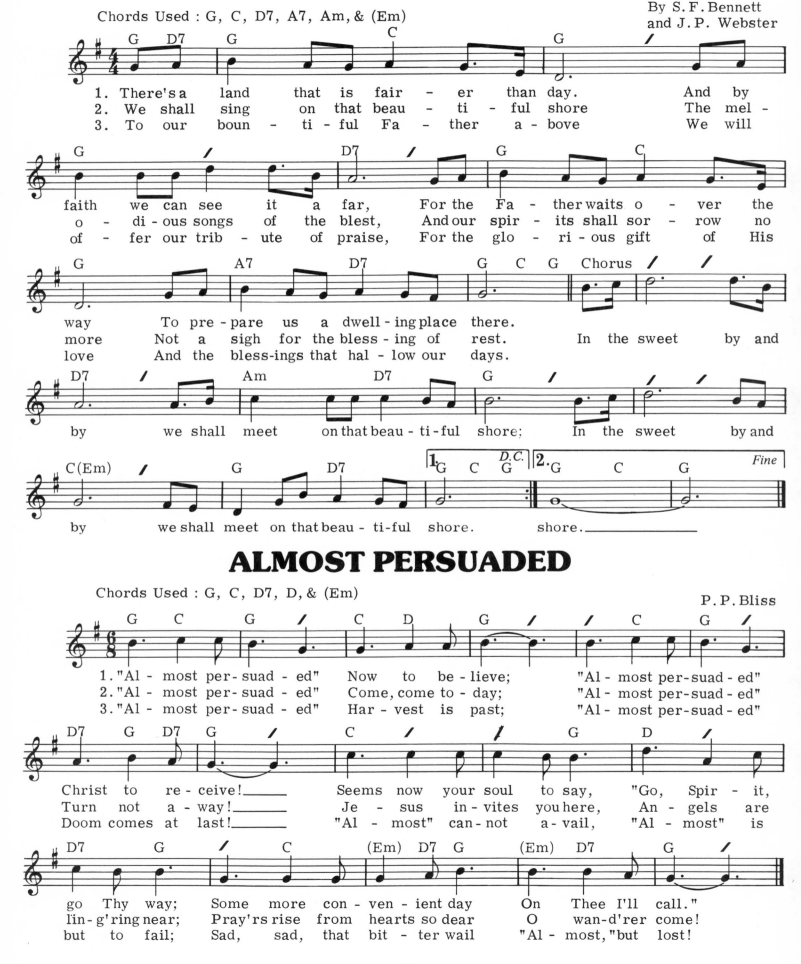

1. There's a land that is fair-er than day. And by
2. We shall sing on that beau-ti-ful shore The mel-
3. To our boun-ti-ful Fa-ther a-bove We will

faith we can see it a-far, For the Fa-ther waits o-ver the
o-di-ous songs of the blest, And our spir-its shall sor-row no
of-fer our trib-ute of praise, For the glo-ri-ous gift of His

way To pre-pare us a dwell-ing place there.
more Not a sigh for the bless-ing of rest. In the sweet by and
love And the bless-ings that hal-low our days.

by we shall meet on that beau-ti-ful shore; In the sweet by and

by we shall meet on that beau-ti-ful shore. shore.

ALMOST PERSUADED

P. P. Bliss

Chords Used : G, C, D7, D, & (Em)

1. "Al-most per-suad-ed" Now to be-lieve; "Al-most per-suad-ed"
2. "Al-most per-suad-ed" Come, come to-day; "Al-most per-suad-ed"
3. "Al-most per-suad-ed" Har-vest is past; "Al-most per-suad-ed"

Christ to re-ceive! Seems now your soul to say, "Go, Spir-it,
Turn not a-way! Je-sus in-vites you here, An-gels are
Doom comes at last! "Al-most" can-not a-vail, "Al-most" is

go Thy way; Some more con-ven-ient day On Thee I'll call."
lin-g'ring near; Pray'rs rise from hearts so dear O wan-d'rer come!
but to fail; Sad, sad, that bit-ter wail "Al-most," but lost!

14

LEANING ON THE EVERLASTING ARMS

Chords Used : G, C, D7, A7, Am, & (Em)

By E. A. Hoffman
and A. J. Showalter

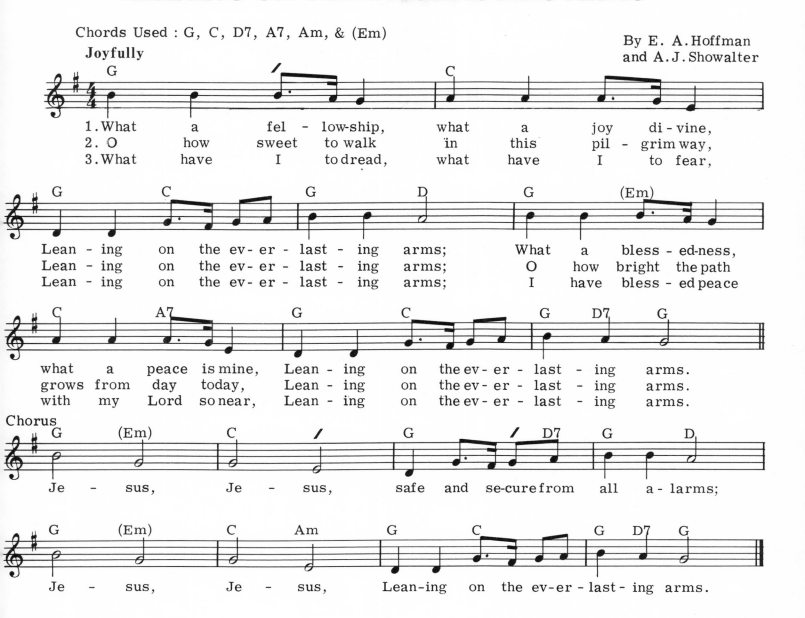

1. What a fel - low-ship, what a joy di - vine,
2. O how sweet to walk in this pil - grim way,
3. What have I to dread, what have I to fear,

Lean - ing on the ev - er - last - ing arms; What a bless - ed-ness,
Lean - ing on the ev - er - last - ing arms; O how bright the path
Lean - ing on the ev - er - last - ing arms; I have bless - ed peace

what a peace is mine, Lean - ing on the ev - er - last - ing arms.
grows from day today, Lean - ing on the ev - er - last - ing arms.
with my Lord so near, Lean - ing on the ev - er - last - ing arms.

Chorus

Je - sus, Je - sus, safe and se-cure from all a - larms;

Je - sus, Je - sus, Lean-ing on the ev - er - last - ing arms.

BLESS THE LORD, O MY SOUL
(PSALM 103:1)

Chords Used : G, C, D7, A7, D & (Em)

Source Unknown

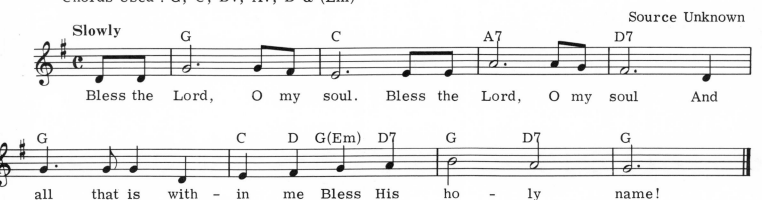

Bless the Lord, O my soul. Bless the Lord, O my soul And

all that is with - in me Bless His ho - ly name!

JESUS, JESUS

Slowly

Source Unknown

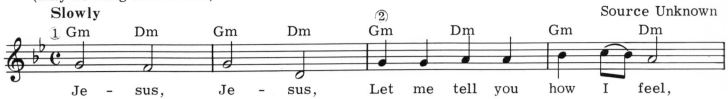

Je - sus, Je - sus, Let me tell you how I feel,

You have giv - en me your rich - es, I love You so. so.

HOW GREAT IS OUR GOD

Chords Used : G, C, D7, A7 & (Em)

How great is our God,_____ How great is His Name.

How great is our God_____ for ev - er the same!

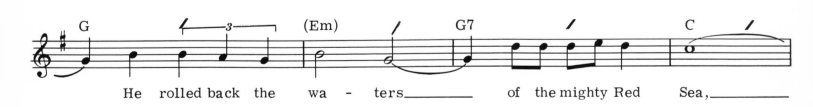

He rolled back the wa - ters_____ of the mighty Red Sea,_____

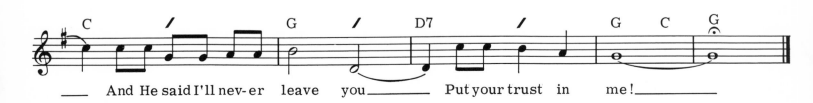

__ And He said I'll nev - er leave you_____ Put your trust in me!_____

16

WE'RE MARCHING TO ZION

Isaac Watts
and
Robert Lowry

ONLY TRUST HIM

Chords Used : G, C, D7, A7, (Em)

J.H.Stockton

1. Come, ev - 'ry soul by sin oppressed There's mer - cy with the Lord,
2. For Je - sus shed His pre - cious blood Rich bless-ings to be stow;
3. Yes, Je - sus is the Truth, the Way, That leads you in - to rest;

And He will sure - ly give you rest By trust-ing in his word.
Plunge now in - to the crim - son flood That wash-es white as snow.
Be - lieve in Him with - out de-lay And you are ful - ly blest.

Chorus

On - ly trust Him, on - ly trust Him, On - ly trust Him now;
He will save you, He will save you, He will
save you now.

COME AND GO WITH ME
(TO MY FATHER'S HOUSE)

Chords Used : G, C, & D7

Lively tempo

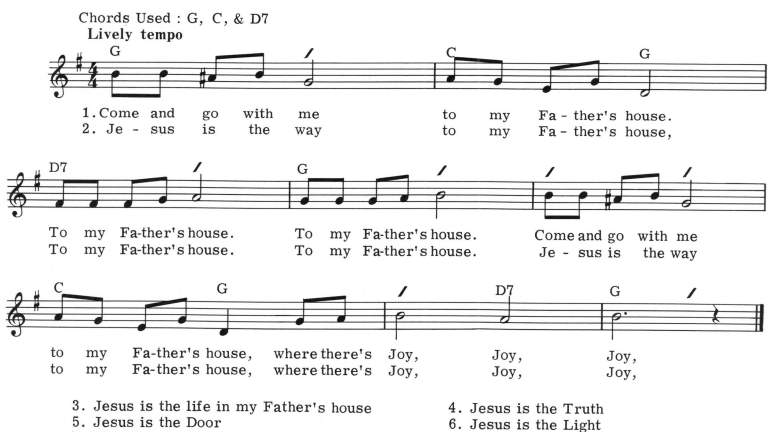

1. Come and go with me to my Fa - ther's house.
2. Je - sus is the way to my Fa - ther's house,

To my Fa-ther's house. To my Fa-ther's house. Come and go with me
To my Fa-ther's house. To my Fa-ther's house. Je - sus is the way

to my Fa-ther's house, where there's Joy, Joy, Joy,
to my Fa-ther's house, where there's Joy, Joy, Joy,

3. Jesus is the life in my Father's house
4. Jesus is the Truth
5. Jesus is the Door
6. Jesus is the Light
7. We will praise the Lord
8. We will raise our hands
9. We will sing and dance

TILL THE POWER COMES DOWN

Chords Used : G, C, D7, G7, A7, & (Em)

Lively tempo   Source Unknown

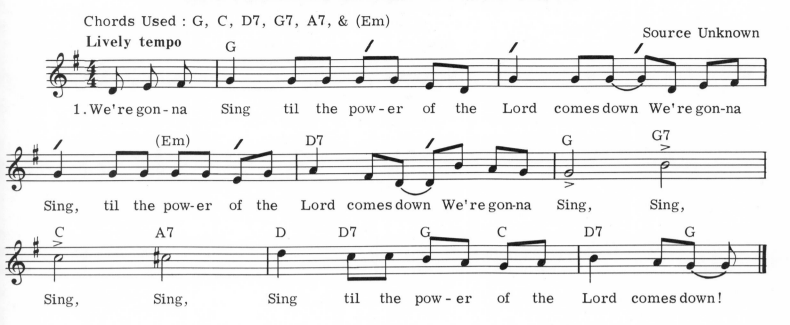

1. We're gon-na Sing til the pow-er of the Lord comes down We're gon-na

Sing, til the pow-er of the Lord comes down We're gon-na Sing, Sing,

Sing, Sing, Sing til the pow-er of the Lord comes down!

2. We're gonna Clap til the power, etc.
3. We will Rejoice when the power of the Lord comes down, etc.
4. We will give Praise when the power of the Lord comes down, etc.

PRAISE TO THE LORD

Chords Used : G, D, C, & D7

Joachim Neander, 1650-80
Tr. Catherine Winkworth, 1892-78   Stralsund Gesangbuch, 1665

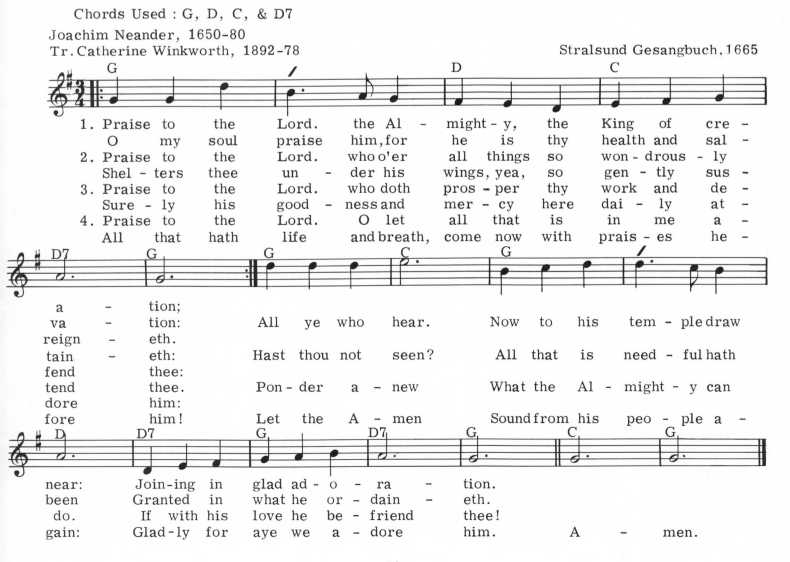

1. Praise to the Lord, the Al - might-y, the King of cre -
   O my soul praise him, for he is thy health and sal -
2. Praise to the Lord, who o'er all things so won - drous - ly
   Shel - ters thee un - der his wings, yea, so gen - tly sus -
3. Praise to the Lord, who doth pros - per thy work and de -
   Sure - ly his good - ness and mer - cy here dai - ly at -
4. Praise to the Lord, O let all that is in me a -
   All that hath life and breath, come now with prais - es he -

a - tion;
va - tion: All ye who hear. Now to his tem - ple draw
reign - eth.
tain - eth: Hast thou not seen? All that is need - ful hath
fend thee:
tend thee. Pon - der a - new What the Al - might - y can
dore him:
fore him! Let the A - men Sound from his peo - ple a -

near: Join-ing in glad ad - o - ra - tion.
been Granted in what he or - dain - eth.
do. If with his love he be - friend thee!
gain: Glad-ly for aye we a - dore him. A - men.

19

MY LORD, MY STRENGTH

Chords Used : Am, G, C, Dm, E7, (Em)

By Bill Bay

1. I shall love Thee O Lord, my strengh.
2. I shall serve Thee O Lord, my strengh.
3. I shall sing of my Lord, my strengh.

And I'll glo-ri-fy Thy name. In your courts I shall
And my end-less praise I give. You have giv-en new
And I lift my hands in praise. Pre-cious is your sweet

walk with thanks giv-ing of your grace shall I pro-claim.
life and sal-va-tion I will bless Thee e'er I live.
oint-ment poured forth. I'll glo-ri-fy you all my days.

© 1973 by Mel Bay Publications, Inc.

Disregard the numbers and arrows. After you have studied the Melody Section (p. 35-50), come back and play melody on this song.

LET US BREAK BREAD TOGETHER

Chords Used : C, F, G7, G, D7, A7, Dm, Am, & (Em)

Moderately

1. Let us break bread to-geth-er on our knees, (on our

knees) Let us break bread to-geth-er on our knees (on our

knees) When I fall on my knees with my face to the ris-ing

sun, O Lord, Have mer-cy on me!

2. Let us drink wine together on our knees, etc.
3. Let us bow 'round the altar on our knees, etc.
4. Let us praise God together on our knees, etc.

20

I WILL FOLLOW HIM
(21 CHORD MODEL)

Chords Used : Dm, G7, C, C7, Gm, A7, A, D7 & B♭

Bill Bay

1. I will fol-low Him where He leads me. With my Lord I'll go,
2. I shall tell of Him where He leads me. By God's Spirit they'll know

I will fol - low Him, sav-ing souls from sin. I love Him so. grow.
that He died for us and He lives for us, His truth shall

Serv - ing the Lord, Christ Je - sus the King! He is the way, His

praise I will sing! The good Shep-herd leads and strengthens me, In His name I shall

go. Sav-ior Je - sus, Lamb of God,___ I love you so.

I'VE GOT PEACE LIKE A RIVER

Chords Used : G, D, A7, D7, G7 & C

Joyfully

1. I've got peace like a riv - er, I've got peace like a riv - er, I've got
2. I've got joy like a foun-tain, I've got joy like a foun-tain, I've got
3. I've got love like an o-cean, I've got love like an o-cean, I've got

peace like a riv - er in my soul; I've got peace like a riv - er, I've got
joy like a foun-tain in my soul, etc.
love like an o-cean in my soul, etc.

peace like a riv - er, I've got peace like a riv - er in my soul.

I LIFT UP MY HANDS IN THY NAME
(MATTHEW 11:28-30 — PSALM 63)

Chords Used : C, F, G7, E7, G, Am & Dm

Bill Bay

Moderately

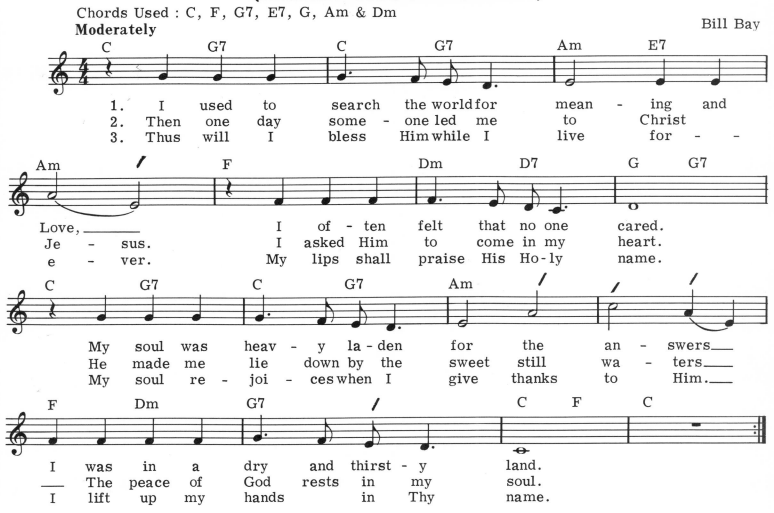

1. I used to search the world for mean - ing and
2. Then one day some - one led me to Christ
3. Thus will I bless Him while I live for - -

Love, _____ I of - ten felt that no one cared.
Je - sus. I asked Him to come in my heart.
e - ver. My lips shall praise His Ho - ly name.

My soul was heav - y la - den for the an - swers___
He made me lie down by the sweet still wa - ters___
My soul re - joi - ces when I give thanks to Him.___

I was in a dry and thirst - y land.
___ The peace of God rests in my soul.
I lift up my hands in Thy name.

PRAISE HIM IN THE MORNING
(21 CHORD MODEL)

Chords Used : G, C, D7, Am, A7, B7, & Em

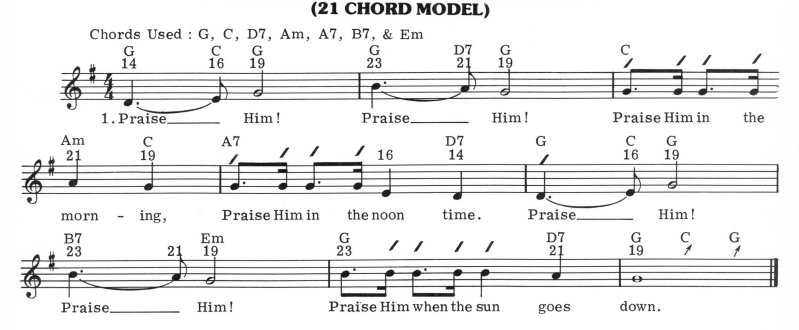

1. Praise___ Him! Praise___ Him! Praise Him in the

morn - ing, Praise Him in the noon time. Praise___ Him!

Praise___ Him! Praise Him when the sun goes down.

2. Love Him ...
3. Trust Him ...
4. Serve Him ...
5. Jesus ...

HALLELUJAH

Chords Used : G, C, D7, D, Am

Hal-le - lu, hal-le-lu, hal-le - lu, hal-le-lu - jah! Praise ye the Lord!

Hal-le - lu, hal-le-lu, hal-le - lu, hal-le-lu - jah! Praise ye the Lord!

Praise ye the Lord, hal-le-lu - jah! Praise ye the Lord, hal-le-lu - jah!

Praise ye the Lord, hal-le-lu - jah! Praise ye the Lord!

PEACE I GIVE YOU
(21 CHORD MODEL)

Chords Used : G, Em, C, A7, D7, Am, B7, & Em

Slowly

Bill Bay

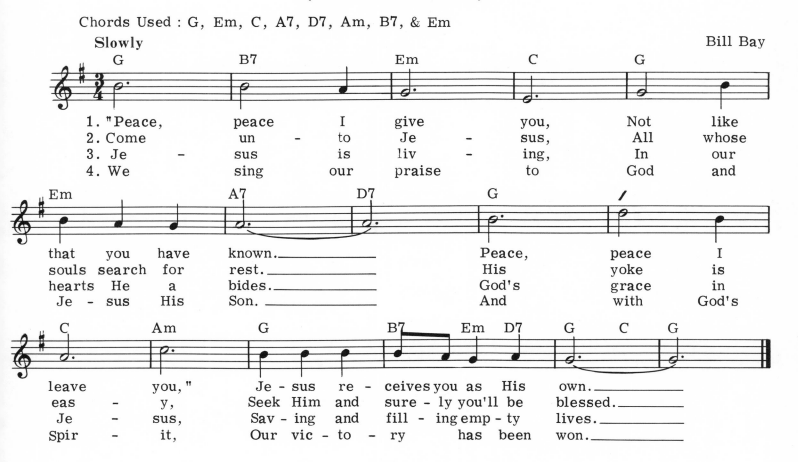

1. "Peace, peace I give you, Not like
2. Come un - to Je - sus, All whose
3. Je - sus is liv - ing, In our
4. We sing our praise to God and

that you have known._____ Peace, peace I
souls search for rest._____ His yoke is
hearts He a bides._____ God's grace in
Je - sus His Son. _____ And with God's

leave you," Je - sus re - ceives you as His own._____
eas - y, Seek Him and sure - ly you'll be blessed._____
Je - sus, Sav - ing and fill - ing emp - ty lives._____
Spir - it, Our vic - to - ry has been won._____

HOLY SPIRIT, DWELL IN ME

Chords used : C, F, G7, C7, Am, Dm

Bill Bay

JESUS IS THE SWEETEST NAME I KNOW

Chords Used : D, G, A7, & (Em)

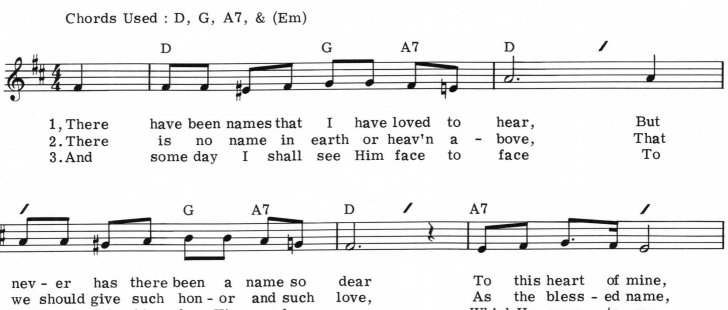

1. There have been names that I have loved to hear, But
2. There is no name in earth or heav'n a - bove, That
3. And some day I shall see Him face to face To

nev - er has there been a name so dear   To this heart of mine,
we should give such hon - or and such love,   As the bless - ed name,
thank and praise him for His won-drous grace,   Which He gave to me,

as the name di-vine,   The pre-cious, precious name of Je - sus.
let us all acclaim,   That wondrous, glo-rious name of Je - sus.
when He made me free,   The bless-ed Son of God called Je - sus.

Chorus

Je - sus is the sweet - est name I know,   And He's

just the same   as His love - ly name,   And that's the rea-son why I love Him

so;   Oh;   Je - sus is the sweet-est name I know.

25

TAKE MY LIFE AND LET IT BE
(21 CHORD MODEL)

Chords used: D, A, A7, G, B7, Em

Swedish Folk Melody

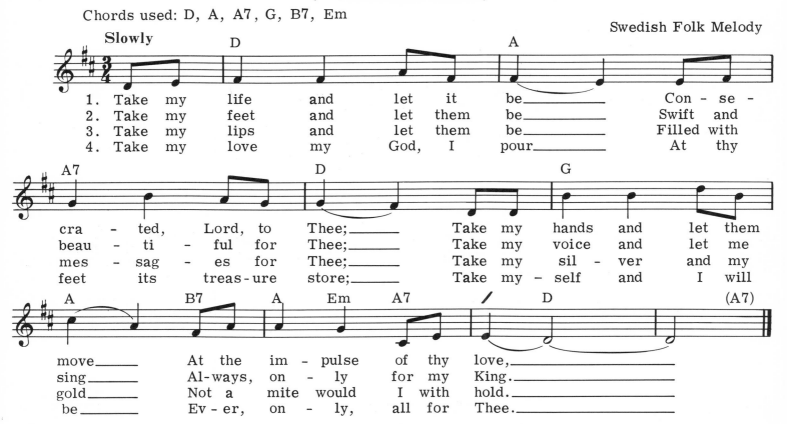

1. Take my life and let it be Con - se -
2. Take my feet and let them be Swift and
3. Take my lips and let them be Filled with
4. Take my love my God, I pour At thy

cra - ted, Lord, to Thee; Take my hands and let them
beau - ti - ful for Thee; Take my voice and let me
mes - sag - es for Thee; Take my sil - ver and my
feet its treas - ure store; Take my - self and I will

move At the im - pulse of thy love,
sing Al - ways, on - ly for my King.
gold Not a mite would I with hold.
be Ev - er, on - ly, all for Thee.

JESUS BREAKS EVERY FETTER
(21 CHORD MODEL)

Chords used: A, D, E7

Moderately

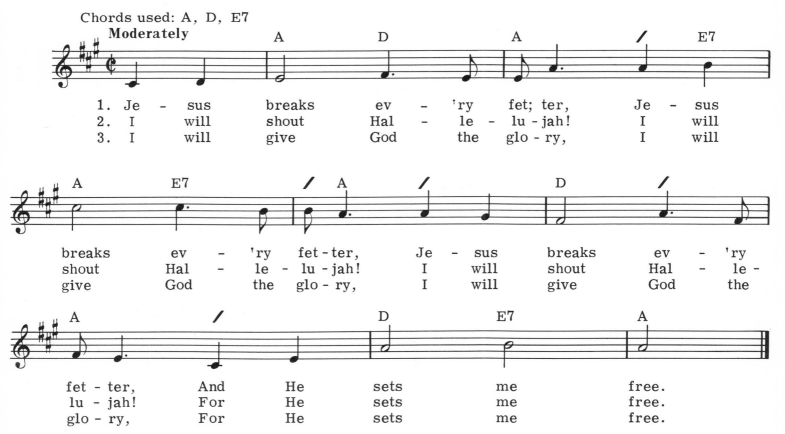

1. Je - sus breaks ev - 'ry fet; ter, Je - sus
2. I will shout Hal - le - lu -jah! I will
3. I will give God the glo - ry, I will

breaks ev - 'ry fet - ter, Je - sus breaks ev - 'ry
shout Hal - le - lu - jah! I will shout Hal - le -
give God the glo - ry, I will give God the

fet - ter, And He sets me free.
lu - jah! For He sets me free.
glo - ry, For He sets me free.

IN THE SPIRIT OF GOD

Chords used: D, C, F

Joyfully, With spirit

Bill Bay

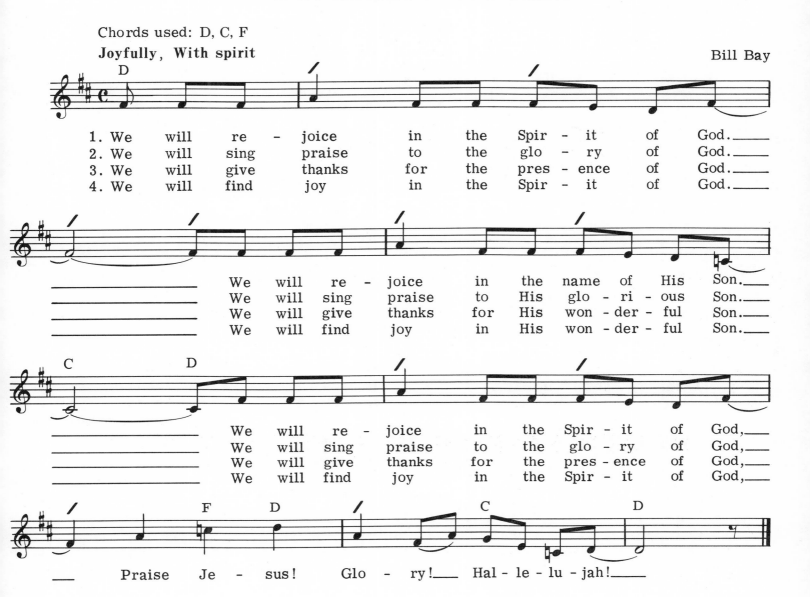

1. We will re - joice in the Spir - it of God.
2. We will sing praise to the glo - ry of God.
3. We will give thanks for the pres - ence of God.
4. We will find joy in the Spir - it of God.

We will re - joice in the name of His Son.
We will sing praise to His glo - ri - ous Son.
We will give thanks for His won - der - ful Son.
We will find joy in His won - der - ful Son.

We will re - joice in the Spir - it of God,
We will sing praise to the glo - ry of God,
We will give thanks for the pres - ence of God,
We will find joy in the Spir - it of God,

Praise Je - sus! Glo - ry! Hal - le - lu - jah!

5. We will find peace in the Spirit of God,
   We will find peace in His wonderful Son.
   We will find peace in the Spirit of God,
   Praise Jesus! Glory! Hallelujah!

6. We will find love in the Spirit of God.
   We will find love in His wonderful Son.
   We will find love in the Spirit of God,
   Praise Jesus! Glory! Hallelujah!

7. We're gonna trust in the Spirit of God.
   We're gonna trust in His wonderful Son.
   We're gonna trust in the Spirit of God,
   Praise Jesus! Glory! Hallelujah!

8. We are one in the Spirit of God.
   We are one with His wonderful Son.
   We are one in the Spirit of God,
   Praise Jesus! Glory! Hallelujah!

JESUS IS HIS NAME

Bill Bay

Chords used: C, G, Dm, F, Am, G7, E7, & A7

1. Al - might - y God, Ev - er-last - ing Fa - ther,
2. Light of the world, Rock of Sal - va - tion,
3. Bright Morn - ing star, His Ho - ly one
4. Re - deem - er, Al - pha and O - me - ga,

Won - der - ful coun-se -lor, Prince of Peace.
Im - man - u - el, Bless-ed Lamb of God.
Res - sur -rec-tion and the Life, The Mes - si - ah.
The word made flesh, Je - sus is His name.

Door of the sheep, Son of God, The
Ser - vant of God, Lord of Hosts, The

Way, Truth and Life, Je - sus is His name.
Bread of Life, Je - sus is His name.

© 1972 by Mel Bay Publications, Inc.

HEAVENLY FATHER, WE APPRECIATE YOU
(21 CHORD MODEL)

Chords used: G, C, B7, Em, Cm, & D7

1. Heav'n-ly Fa - ther we ap - pre - ci - ate you.
2. Son of God, I mag - ni - fy you,
3. Ho - ly Spir - it what a com - fort you are,

Heav'n-ly Fa - ther, we ap - pre - ci - ate you.
Son of God, I mag - ni - fy you,
Ho - ly Spir - it what a com - fort you are,

We love you, a - dore you, we bow down be -
You've cleansed me from sin, and sent the Spir - it with -
You lead us, you guide us, you live right in -

fore you, Heav'n-ly Fa - ther we ap-pre - ci - ate you.
in. Son of God, I mag - ni - fy you.
side us, Ho - ly Spir - it what a com - fort you are.

© 1972 by Mel Bay Publications, Inc.

OH, HOW I LOVE JESUS

Chords used: F, B , C7, A7, Dm, & Gm

Oh, how I love Je - sus, Oh, how I love Je - sus,___

Oh, how I love Je - sus, be - cause__ He first loved me.___

To me He is so won-der-ful,___ To me He is so won - der - ful, To

me He is so wonderful,___ Be - cause__ He first loved me.___

D.C.

I SEE THE LORD
(21 CHORD MODEL)

Chords used: G, C7, D7, B7, A7, Em

1. I see the Lord, I see the Lord! He is
2. I see the Lord, I see the Lord! And His

high and lift-ed up, and His train fills the Tem-ple, He is high and lift - ed up, and His
eyes are like the Fire, and His Face Like the Lightning! And His eyes are like the Fire, and His

train fills the Tem-ple! And His an-gels cry, "Ho - ly!" His an-gels cry, "Ho-ly!" His
Face Like the Lightning! And His an-gels cry, "Ho - ly!" The an-gels cry, "Ho-ly!" The

an - gels cry, "Ho - ly is the Lord!"___
an - gels cry, "Holy Un - to the Lord!"___

ALL MY TRIALS

Chords used: C, F, G7, Dm, E7 & C7
Key of F

1. Oh hush lit-tle ba - by, don't you cry,_____ You know your ma - ma_____
2. I've got a lit-tle book with pa - ges three_____ And ev' - ry page_____
3. If liv-ing was a thing that money could buy_____ The rich would live_____
4. There grows a tree in par - a - dise And the pil-grims call it_____

___ was born to die,_____
___ spells li - ber - ty._____   Chorus: All_____ my tri-als,_____
___ but the poor would die._____
___ the tree of life._____

Lord, soon_____ be o - ver_____

Key of F

Too late, my broth-ers;_____ Too late, but never mind._____

ALTERNATE RHYTHM

Chords used: D, D7, A7, E7 & G
Key of G

Key of D

Key of G

Fine

30

BLESSED IS THE MAN
(PSALM 1)

Chords used: G, D, C, D7, (Em)

Bright, moving tempo

By Bill Bay

THE LORD IS MY SHEPHERD
(PSALM 23)

Chords used: C, (Em), F, C, Dm, G7, C7

By Bill Bay

MELODY PLAYING*

The following songs are arranged for melody playing. You will notice that the chord changes are more frequent in order to find the chord that contains both the desired melody note and the proper harmonic background.

Starting with the lowest, thickest string, each string on the Autoharp is numbered from 1 to 36. Each number under the chord designation indicates the location of the melody string to be pinched or strummed. The chord symbol is not repeated until time for a new chord to be played.

To play melody, press down the designated chord bar and strum up to the area of the melody string (or note). This is *melody strumming.* You can also pinch gently with the thumb and index, or thumb and middle finger in the same area. The index or middle finger will be picking the melody string and the thumb will be picking a lower string at the same time, thus adding depth and harmony. This is *melody picking.* The thumb can also make small brush-like strokes on the lower strings whenever necessary to keep the rhythm going. An upstroke, from the lower to the higher strings is shown by this symbol ⟋, and a downstroke, from the higher to the lower strings is ⟍ .

Don't worry about picking the exact string, since several strings are dampened on either side of the melody string. *You are not plucking an open string, but a section of the depressed chord.*

The slash (/) means to repeat the previous melody note and chord. Soon you will be able to play melody just by reading the chord changes and playing by ear. However, at first, it will help to cut out the Melody Aid on p. 56 and tape it under the strings as in fig. 7. The heavy line is placed directly under the lowest string.

Figure 7

*For further study of melody picking see The Many Ways To Play The Autoharp, vol. 2, 1966, Meg Peterson, Oscar Schmidt-International, Inc., Garden State Rd., Union, NJ. 97983; and Teaching Music With The Autoharp, pp. 44-47, Meg Peterson & Robert E. Nye, 1973. Music Education Group, 20 Stern Ave., Springfield, N.J. 07081.

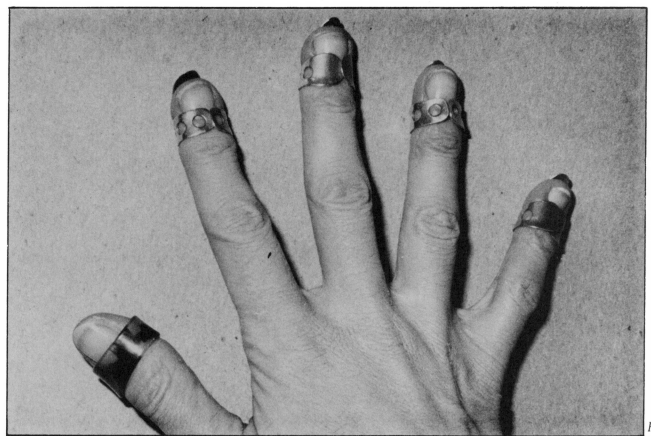

Figure 8

Many players use two finger picks and a thumb pick for melody picking. See how they are worn in the picture.

Try picking out the melody of many of the songs in the first section of this book. Pick out the chords in which the melody note is located and change chords whenever the melody requires it. The 7th chord in a particular key is the one most frequently employed to play passing tones. For example: in the key of C this would be a G7 chord; in the key of F, a C7 chord and in the key of G, a D7 chord.

If you do not need the string numbers, simply ignore them and follow the chord changes only, supplying your own rhythm accompaniment throughout.

As in simple strumming the chords in parenthesis ( ) are optional. If you do not have the optional chord on your particular model Autoharp keep using the previous chord until a change occurs. There are many ways to harmonize a melody. The optional chords are simply more interesting and should be used if you have a 21 chord model (See pg. 00 for pictures of Autoharp models).

Chart for Finding All Notes on the Autoharp

GO, TELL IT ON THE MOUNTAIN

Chords used: C, F, G, G7, D7, E7, & Am

Spiritual

SEARCH ME

Chords used: F, Bb, C7, C, Dm, E7, Gm, & F7

Maori Melody

1. Search me O God, _____ And know my heart to - day; _____ Try me, O Sa - vior, know my thoughts, I pray, _____ See if there be _____ some wick - ed way in me _____ Cleanse me from ev' - ry sin and set me free. _____
2. I praise the Lord _____ for cleans - ing me from sin; _____ Ful - fill my word, and make me pure with - in; _____ Fill me with fire _____ where once I burned with shame; _____ Grant me de - sire to mag - ni - fy Thy name. _____
3. Lord, take my life, _____ and make it whol - ly thine; _____ Fill my poor heart with Thy great love di - vine; _____ Take all my will, _____ my pas - sion, self and pride; _____ I now sur - render, Lord, in me a - bide. _____
4. O Ho - ly Ghost, _____ re - viv - al comes from Thee. _____ Send a re - viv - al, Thy start the work in me. _____ Thy word de - clares, _____ Thou wilt sup - ply our need; _____ For bless - ing now, O Lord, I hum - bly plead. _____

I LOVE THEE

SWING LOW, SWEET CHARIOT

WHAT A FRIEND WE HAVE IN JESUS

HERE COMES JESUS

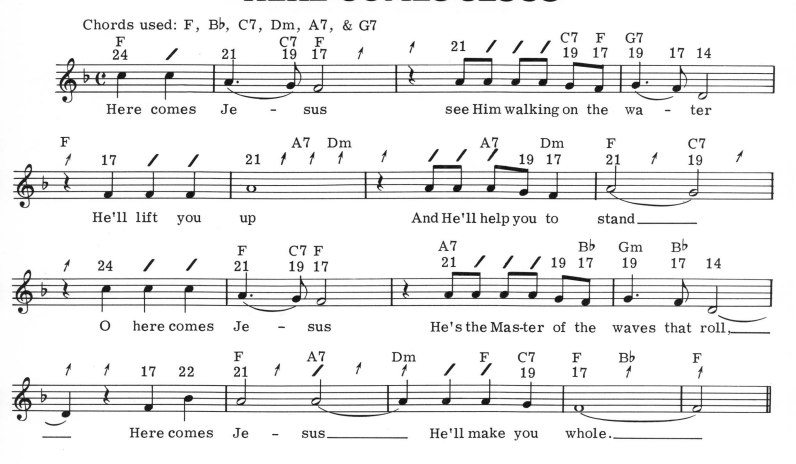

GREAT IS THE LORD

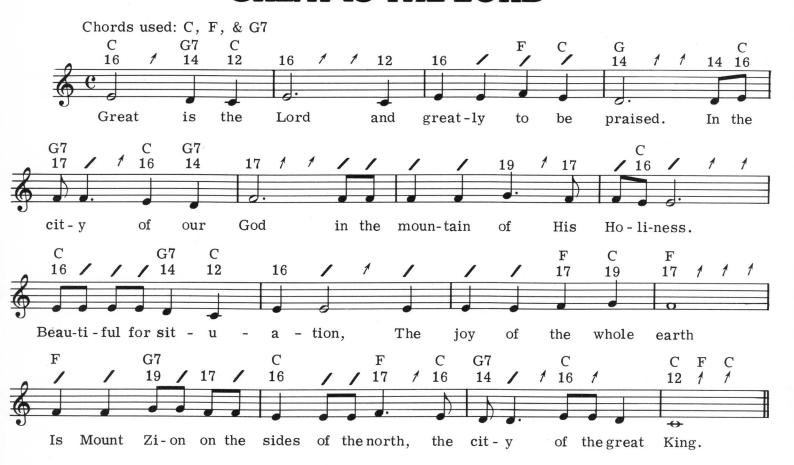

WERE YOU THERE?

Chords used: C, F, & G7

Spiritual

1. Were you there when they cru - ci - fied my Lord?_____
2. Were you there when they nailed Him to the tree? etc._____
3. Were you there when they laid Him in the tomb? etc._____
4. Were you there when He rose up from the tomb?_____

Were you there when they cru - ci - fied my Lord?

Oh_____ some-times it caus - es me to

trem - ble, trem - ble, trem - ble. Were you

there when they cru - ci - fied my Lord?

COME AND GO WITH ME
(TO THAT LAND)

Chords used: C, G, D7, G7, Am, & (Em)

OH, IT IS JESUS

Chords used: C, F, & G7

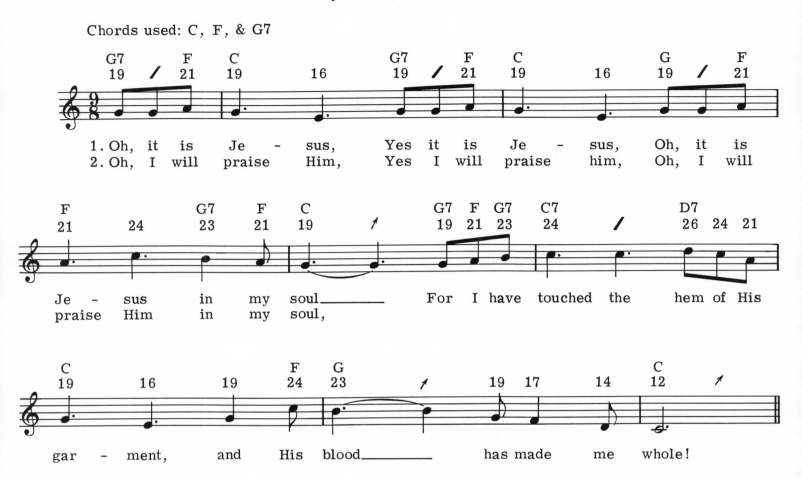

1. Oh, it is Je - sus, Yes it is Je - sus, Oh, it is Je - sus in my soul_____ For I have touched the hem of His gar - ment, and His blood_____ has made me whole!
2. Oh, I will praise Him, Yes I will praise him, Oh, I will praise Him in my soul,

I LOVE HIM

Chords used: C, F, & G7

I love Him,_ I love Him,_ be - cause He first loved me. And pur - chased my sal - va - tion on Cal - v'ry's tree.

LONESOME VALLEY

Chords used: G, B♭, & C7

1. Je - sus walked_____ this lone - some val - ley,_____ He had to
2. We must walk_____ this lone - some val - ley,_____ We have to
3. You must go_____ and stand your tri - al,_____ You have to

walk_____ it by Him - self, Oh, no - bod - y else_____ could walk it
walk_____ it by our - selves Oh, no - bod - y else_____ can walk it
stand_____ it by your - self, Oh, no - bod - y else_____ can stand your

for Him He had to walk it by him - self._____
for us, We have to walk it by our - selves.____
tri - al, You have to stand it by your - self.____

THY LOVING KINDNESS
(PSALM 63:3-4)

Chords used: D, A7, G, (Em)

Moderately

Thy lov - ing kind - ness_____ is bet - ter than life,
I lift my hands up_____ un - to____ Thy name,

Thy lov - ing kind - ness_____ is bet - ter than life.
I life my hands up_____ un - to____ Thy name.

My lips shall praise Thee_____ Thus will I bless Thee
My lips shall praise Thee_____ Thus will I bless Thee

I will lift up my hands un - to Thy name.
I will lift up my hands un - to Thy name.

KUM BA YAH
(COME BY HERE)

Chords used; C, F, G7, G, & Dm

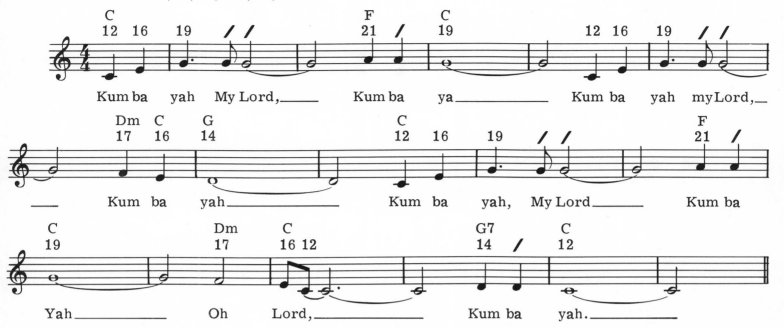

AMAZING GRACE

Chords used: G, C, D7, G7, & (Em)

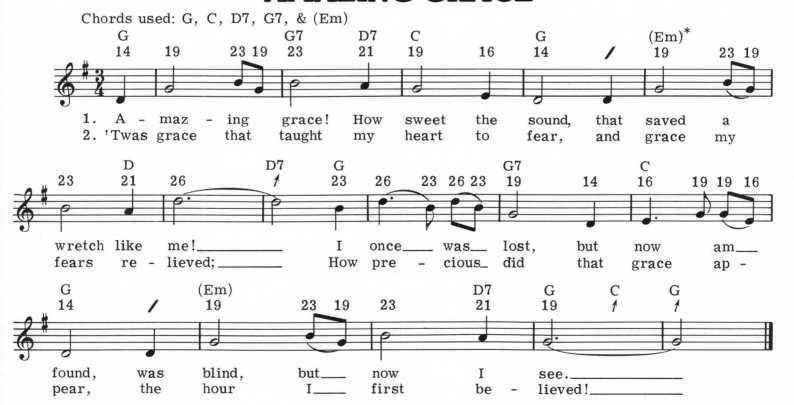

3. Through many dangers, toils and snares
I have already come;
'Tis grace hath brought me safe thus far,
And grace will lead me home.

4. When we've been there ten thousand years,
Bright shining as the sun,
We've no less days to sing God's praise
Than when we first begun.

5. Alleluia, Alleluia, Alleluia, Praise God! (Repeat)

* Chords in parenthesis are optional. If the player does not have a 21 chord model, continue to use the G chord.

BLESSED BE THE NAME

Chords used: G, C, D7, & D

1. Bless-ed be the Name, Bless-ed be the Name,
2. Je-sus is the name, Je-sus is the name,

Bless-ed be the name of the Lord. Bless-ed be the name,
Je-sus is the name of the Lord. Je-sus is the name,

Blessed be the name, Bless-ed be the Name of the Lord.
Je-sus is the name, Je-sus is the name of the Lord.

Vs. 3. Worthy is the name
Vs. 4. Holy is the name

PRAISE HIM IN THE MORNING
(21 CHORD MODEL)

Chords used: G, C, D7, Am, A7, B7, & Em

1. Praise_____ Him! Praise_____ Him! Praise Him in the

morn-ing, Praise Him in the noon-time. Praise_____ Him!

Praise_____ Him! Praise Him when the sun goes down.

2. Love Him...
3. Trust Him...
4. Serve Him...
5. Jesus...

TO GOD BE THE GLORY

Chords used: G, C, D7, A7, D, Am, & (B7)

1. To God be the glo-ry, great things He hath done; So loved He the world that He gave us His Son, Who yield - ed His life an a - tone - ment for sin, And o - pened the life gate that all may go in.

2. O per - fect re - demp-tion, the pur-chase of blood, To ev'- ry be - liev - er the prom - ise of God; The vil - est of - fend - er who tru - ly be - lieves, That mo - ment from Je - sus a par - don re - ceives.

3. Great things he hath taught us, great things He hath done, And great our re - joic - ing thru Je - sus the Son; But pur - er and high - er and great - er will be Our won - der, our trans - port when Je - sus we see.

REFRAIN
Praise the Lord, praise the Lord, Let the earth hear His voice! Praise the Lord, praise the Lord, Let the peo - ple re - joice! O come to the Fa - ther, through Je - sus the Son, And give Him the glo - ry, great things He hath done.

OH, SINNER MAN
(21 CHORD MODEL)

Chords used: Em, D, B7, C, A, G

4. Run to the moon, the moon was a-bleeding, (3 times)
   All on that day.

5. Run to the Lord, Lord won't you hide me? (3 times)
   All on that day.

6, Run to the Devil, Devil was a -waiting;   (3 times)
   All on that day.

7. Oh, sinner man, you oughta been a-praying, (3 times)
   All on that day.

8. Oh, sinner man, you should have found Jesus;(3 times)
   Long before that day.

JACOB'S LADDER

Chords used: C, G, F, G7, C7

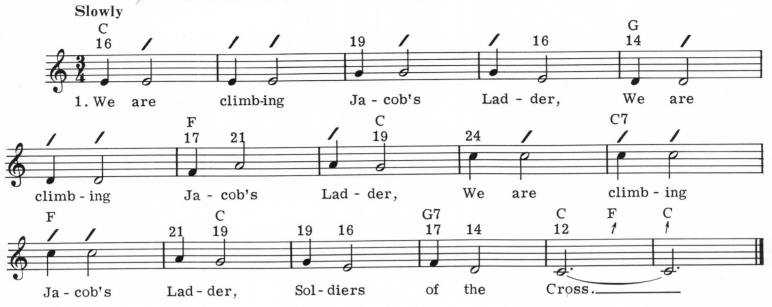

Slowly

1. We are climb-ing Ja-cob's Lad-der, We are climb-ing Ja-cob's Lad-der, We are climb-ing Ja-cob's Lad-der, Sol-diers of the Cross._____

2. Every round goes higher, higher, (3 times)
   Soldier of the cross.

3. Sinner, do you love my Jesus? (3 times)
   Soldier of the cross.

4. If you love Him, why not serve him? (3 times)
   Soldier of the cross.

5. We are climbing higher, higher, (3 times)
   Soldier of the cross.

6. Rise, Shine, give God glory, (3 times)
   Soldier of the cross.

LORD, I WANT TO BE A CHRISTIAN

Chords used: D, G, A7, D7,(B7)

Spiritual

Brightly

1. Lord, I want to be a Chris-tian in-a my heart, in-a my heart, Lord I want to be a Christian in-a my heart,_____ In-a my heart_____ in-a my heart,_____ Lord I want to be a Chris-tian in-a my heart._____

2. Lord, I want to be more loving in-a my heart, etc...
3. Lord, I want to be more holy in-a my heart, etc...
4. Lord, I want to be like Jesus in-a my heart, etc...

THERE IS POWER IN THE BLOOD
(21 CHORD MODEL)

Chords used: A, D, & E7

MICHAEL ROW THE BOAT ASHORE

Chords used: C, F, Dm, G7, (Em)

Spiritual

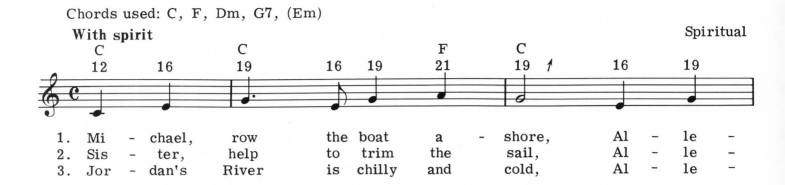

1. Mi - chael, row the boat a - shore, Al - le -
2. Sis - ter, help to trim the sail, Al - le -
3. Jor - dan's River is chilly and cold, Al - le -

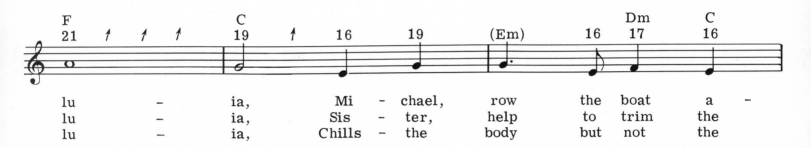

lu - ia, Mi - chael, row the boat a -
lu - ia, Sis - ter, help to trim the
lu - ia, Chills - the body but not the

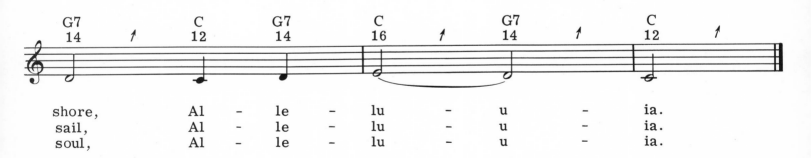

shore, Al - le - lu - u - ia.
sail, Al - le - lu - u - ia.
soul, Al - le - lu - u - ia.

4. Jordan's River is deep and wide,
   Hallelujah!
   Milk and honey on the other side,
   Hallelujah!

5. I have heard the good news too,
   Hallelujah!
   I have heard the good news too,
   Hallelujah!

6. Repeat verse one

53

ALL HAIL THE POWER OF JESUS' NAME
(21 CHORD MODEL)

BLESSED ASSURANCE

Melody Aids*

*Used by permission of Music Education Group, Union N.J. From "Teaching Music With The Autoharp,"Robert E. Nye, Meg Peterson.

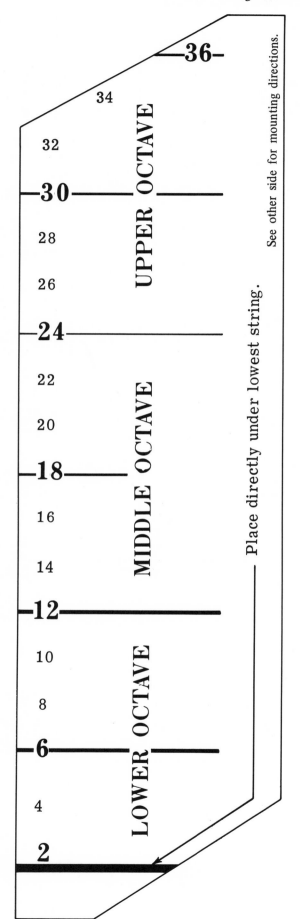

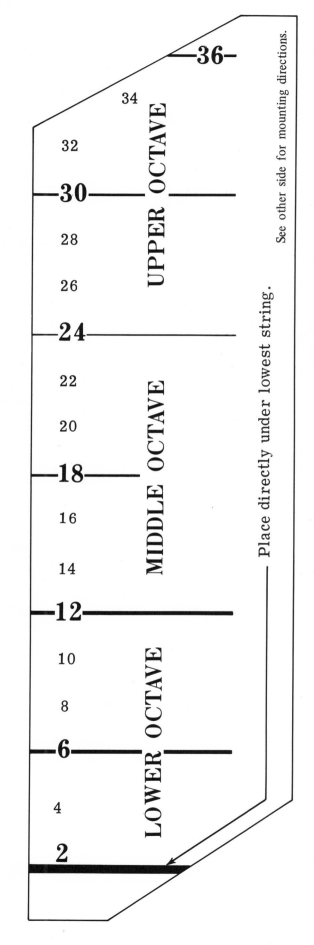